# Born in 1976

# By

# Kerry Butters.

# Born in 1976

**Millennium:**            2nd millennium

**Centuries:**    19th century – **20th century** – 21st century

**Decades:**    1940s 1950s 1960s – **1970s** – 1980s 1990s
2000s

**Years:**        1973 1974 1975 – **1976** – 1977 1978 1979

**1976 (MCMLXXVI)** was a leap year starting on Thursday (dominical letter DC) of the Gregorian calendar, the 1976th year of the Common Era (CE) and *Anno Domini* (AD) designations, the 976th year of the 2nd millennium, the 76th year of the 20th century, and the 7th year of the 1970s decade.

# Contents

# Events

## January

- January – The Cray-1, the first commercially developed supercomputer, is released by Seymour Cray's Cray Research.
- January 5 – The Pol Pot regime proclaims a new constitution for Democratic Kampuchea.
- January 11 – The 1976 Philadelphia Flyers–Red Army game results in a 4–1 victory for the National Hockey League's Philadelphia Flyers over HC CSKA Moscow of the Soviet Union.
- January 15 – Would-be Gerald Ford presidential assassin Sara Jane Moore is sentenced to life in prison.
- January 16 – The trial against jailed members of the Red Army Faction begins in Stuttgart, West Germany.
- January 18

- Full diplomatic relations are established between Bangladesh and Pakistan 5 years after the Bangladesh Liberation War.
- The Scottish Labour Party is formed.
- Super Bowl X: The Pittsburgh Steelers defeat the Dallas Cowboys, 21–17, in Miami.
- January 19 – Jimmy Carter wins the Iowa Democratic Caucus.
- January 21 – The first commercial *Concorde* flight takes off.
- January 27
  - The United States vetoes a United Nations resolution that calls for an independent Palestinian state.
  - The First Battle of Amgala breaks out between Morocco and Algeria in the Spanish Sahara.
- January 29 – Twelve Provisional Irish Republican Army bombs explode in the West End of London.
- January 30 – *Live from Lincoln Center* debuts on PBS.

## February

- February 4
  - The 1976 Winter Olympics begin in Innsbruck, Austria.

- In Guatemala and Honduras an earthquake kills more than 22,000.
- February 5 – Nearly 2,000 students become involved in a racially charged riot at Escambia High School in Pensacola, Florida; 30 students are injured in the 4-hour fray.
- February 9 – The Australian Defence Force is formed by unification of the Australian Army, the Royal Australian Navy and the Royal Australian Air Force.
- February 11 – Clifford Alexander, Jr. is confirmed as the first African American Secretary of the United States Army.
- February 13 – General Murtala Mohammed of Nigeria is assassinated in a military coup.
- February 15 – The 1976 Constitution of Cuba is adopted by national referendum.
- February 24 – Cuba's current constitution is enacted.
- February 26 – The Spanish Armed Forces withdraw from Western Sahara.
- February 27 – The Polisario Front, Western Sahara's national liberation movement, declares independence of the territory under the name "Sahrawi Arab Democratic Republic".
- February 28 – Madagascar becomes the first country to recognise the Sahrawi Arab Democratic Republic.

# March

- March 1
  - U.K. Home Secretary Merlyn Rees ends Special Category Status for those sentenced for scheduled terrorist crimes relating to the civil violence in Northern Ireland.
  - Burundi recognizes the Sahrawi Arab Democratic Republic (SADR).
- March 2 – Vietnam recognizes the Sahrawi Arab Democratic Republic (SADR).
- March 4
  - The Maguire Seven are found guilty of possessing explosives and subsequently jailed for 14 years.
  - The Northern Ireland Constitutional Convention is formally dissolved in Northern Ireland, resulting in direct rule of Northern Ireland from London via the British Parliament.
- March 6 – Algeria recognizes the Sahrawi Arab Democratic Republic (SADR).
- March 9 – A cable car disaster in Cavalese, Italy leaves 42 dead.
- March 9 – March 11 – Two coal mine explosions claim 26 lives at the Blue Diamond Coal Co. Scotia Mine, in Letcher County, Kentucky.

- March 11 – Angola and Benin recognize the Sahrawi Arab Democratic Republic (SADR).
- March 13 – Mozambique recognizes the Sahrawi Arab Democratic Republic (SADR).
- March 14 – After eight years on NBC, *The Wizard of Oz* returns to CBS, where it will remain until 1999, setting what was likely then a record for the most telecasts of a Hollywood film on a commercial television network. That record is broken by *The Ten Commandments* in 1996, which began its annual network telecasts on ABC in 1973 and is still (as of 2012) telecast by that network.
- March 15 – Guinea-Bissau recognizes the Sahrawi Arab Democratic Republic (SADR).
- March 16
  - Harold Wilson resigns as Prime Minister of the United Kingdom.
  - North Korea recognizes the Sahrawi Arab Democratic Republic (SADR).
- March 17
  - Rubin "Hurricane" Carter is retried in New Jersey.
  - Togo recognizes the Sahrawi Arab Democratic Republic (SADR).
- March 20 – Patty Hearst is found guilty of armed robbery of a San Francisco bank.

- March 24
  - Argentina military forces depose president Isabel Perón.
  - A general strike takes place in the People's Republic of the Congo.
- March 26 – The Toronto Blue Jays are created.
- March 27 – The first 4.6 miles of the Washington Metro subway system open.
- March 29 – The military dictatorship of General Jorge Videla comes to power in Argentina.
- March 31 – The New Jersey Supreme Court rules that coma patient Karen Ann Quinlan can be disconnected from her ventilator. She remains comatose and dies in 1985.

## April

- April 1
  - Apple Computer Company is formed by Steve Jobs and Steve Wozniak.
  - Conrail (Consolidated Rails Corporation) is formed by the U.S. government, to take control of 13 major Northeast Class-1 railroads that had filed for bankruptcy protection. Conrail takes control at midnight, as a government-owned and operated railroad until 1986, when it is sold to the public.

- The Jovian–Plutonian gravitational effect is first reported by astronomer Patrick Moore.
- Rwanda recognizes the Sahrawi Arab Democratic Republic (SADR).
- April 2 – Norodom Sihanouk is forced to resign as Head of State of Kampuchea by the Khmer Rouge led by Pol Pot and is placed under house arrest.
- April 3 – The Eurovision Song Contest 1976 is won by Brotherhood of Man, representing the United Kingdom, with their song "Save Your Kisses for Me".
- April 5
  - James Callaghan becomes Prime Minister of the United Kingdom.
  - Tiananmen Incident: Large crowds lay wreaths at Beijing's *Monument of the Martyrs* to commemorate the death of Premier Zhou Enlai. Poems against the Gang of Four are also displayed, provoking a police crackdown.
- April 10 – *Frampton Comes Alive!*, the multi-platinum selling live album by English rock musician Peter Frampton hits #1 in the *Billboard* 200 and remains there for 10 weeks, becoming the best-selling album of the year.
- April 13
  - An explosion in an ammunition factory in Lapua, Finland kills 40.

- The United States Treasury Department reintroduces the two-dollar bill as a Federal Reserve Note on Thomas Jefferson's 233rd birthday as part of the United States Bicentennial celebration.
- April 16 – As a measure to curb population growth, the minimum age for marriage in India is raised to 21 years for men and 18 years for women.
- April 21 – The Great Bookie Robbery in Melbourne: Bandits steal A$1.4 million in bookmakers' settlements from Queen Street, Melbourne.
- April 23
  - The punk rock group the Ramones release their first self-titled album.
  - Jethro Tull release their album *Too Old to Rock 'n' Roll: Too Young to Die!*.
- April 25 – Portugal's new constitution is enacted.
- April 29 – Sino-Soviet split: A concealed bomb explodes at the gates of the Soviet embassy in China, killing four Chinese. The targets were embassy employees, returning from lunch, but on that day they returned to the embassy earlier.

## May

- May 1 – Neville Wran becomes Premier of New South Wales.

- May 4
    - The first LAGEOS (Laser Geodynamics Satellite) is launched.
    - A train crash in Schiedam, the Netherlands, kills 24 people.
- May 6 – An earthquake hits the Friuli area in Italy, killing more than 900 people and making another 100,000 homeless.
- May 9 – Ulrike Meinhof of the Red Army Faction is found hanged in an apparent suicide, in her Stuttgart-Stammheim prison cell.
- May 11
    - U.S. President Gerald Ford signs the Federal Election Campaign Act.
    - An accident involving a tanker truck carrying anhydrous ammonia takes place in Houston, Texas, resulting in the deaths of 7 people.
- May 21 – The Yuba City bus disaster, the worst bus crash in U.S. history to date, with 28 students and one teacher killed.
- May 24 – Washington, D.C. Concorde service begins.
- May 25 – U.S. President Gerald Ford defeats challenger Ronald Reagan in 3 Republican presidential primaries: Kentucky, Tennessee and Oregon.

- May 30 – Indianapolis 500-Mile Race: Johnny Rutherford wins the (rain-shortened) shortest race in event history to date, at 102 laps or 255 miles (408 km).
- May 31 – Syria intervenes in the Lebanese Civil War in opposition to the Palestine Liberation Organization, whom it had previously supported.

## June

- June 1 – The UK and Iceland end the Cod War.
- June 2
  - A car bomb fatally injures *Arizona Republic* reporter Don Bolles.
  - The Philippine government opens relations with the Soviet Union.
- June 4 – The Boston Celtics defeat the Phoenix Suns 128–126 in triple overtime in Game 5 of the NBA Finals at the Boston Garden. In 1997, the game is selected by a panel of experts as the greatest of the NBA's first 50 years.
- June 5 – The Teton Dam collapses in southeast Idaho in the U.S., killing 11 people.
- June 6 – The Double Six Crash, a plane crash in Kota Kinabalu, Malaysia, kills everyone on board, including Sabahan Chief Minister Tun Fuad Stephens.

- June 12 – Alberto Demicheli, a jurist, is inaugurated as a civilian de facto President of Uruguay after Juan María Bordaberry is deposed by the military.
- June 13 – Savage thunderstorms roll through the state of Iowa, spawning several tornadoes, including an F-5 tornado that destroys the town of Jordan, Iowa.
- June 14 – The trial begins at Oxford Crown Court of Donald Neilson, the killer known as the Black Panther.
- June 16 – The Soweto uprising in South Africa begins.
- June 17 – The National Basketball Association and the American Basketball Association agree on the ABA–NBA merger.
- June 20
    - Hundreds of Western tourists are moved from Beirut and taken to safety in Syria by the U.S. military, following the murder of the U.S. ambassador.
    - General elections are held in Italy.
    - Czechoslovakia beats West Germany 5–3 on penalties to win Euro 76, when the game had ended 2–2 after extra time.
- June 25 – Strikes start in Poland (Ursus, Radom, Płock) after communists raise food prices; they end on June 30.

- June 26 – The CN Tower is built in Toronto; the tallest free-standing land structure opens to the public.
- June 27
  - G-6 is renamed "Group of 7" (G-7).
  - Palestinian militants hijack an Air France plane in Greece with 246 passengers and 12 crew. They take it to Entebbe, Uganda.
- June 29
  - Seychelles gains independence from the United Kingdom.
  - The Conference of Communist and Workers Parties of Europe convenes in East Berlin.

## July

Italian tall ship Amerigo Vespucci in New York Harbor during the United States Bicentennial celebration.

- July 2 – North Vietnam dissolves the Provisional Government of South Vietnam and unites the two countries to form the Socialist Republic of Vietnam.

- July 3 – *Gregg v. Georgia*: The Supreme Court of the United States rules that the death penalty is not inherently cruel or unusual and is a constitutionally acceptable form of punishment overturning the Furman v. Georgia case of 1972.
- July 3 – The great heat wave in the United Kingdom, which is currently suffering from drought conditions, reaches its peak.
- July 4
  - *United States Bicentennial*: From coast to coast, the United States celebrates the 200th anniversary of the Declaration of Independence.
  - Entebbe Raid: Israeli airborne commandos free 103 hostages being held by Palestinian hijackers of an Air France plane at Uganda's Entebbe Airport; Yonatan Netanyahu and several Ugandan soldiers are killed in the raid.
- July 6 – The first class of women is inducted at the United States Naval Academy in Annapolis, Maryland.
- July 7
  - German left-wing terrorists Monika Berberich, Gabriella Rollnick, Juliane Plambeck and Inge Viett escape from the Lehrter Straße maximum security prison in West Berlin.

- David Steel becomes leader of the UK's Liberal Party in the aftermath of the scandal which forced out Jeremy Thorpe.
- July 10
  - Four mercenaries, three British and one American, are shot by firing squad in Angola.
  - An explosion in Seveso, Italy, causes extended pollution to a large area in the neighborhood of Milano, with many evacuations and a large number of people affected by the toxic cloud.
- July 12 – Barbara Jordan is the first African-American to keynote a political convention.
- July 15 – Jimmy Carter is nominated for U.S. President at the Democratic National Convention in New York City.
- July 16 – July 20 – Albert Spaggiari and his gang break into the vault of the Societe Generale Bank in Nice, France.
- July 17
  - The 1976 Summer Olympics begin in Montreal, Canada.
  - East Timor is declared the 27th province of Indonesia.
- July 18 – Nadia Comăneci earns the first of 7 perfect scores of 10 at the 1976 Summer Olympics.

- July 19 – Sagarmatha National Park in Nepal is created.
- July 20 – Viking program: The Viking 1 lander successfully lands on Mars.
- July 21 – A bomb kills Christopher Ewart-Biggs, British ambassador to the Irish Republic.
- July 26 – In Los Angeles, Ronald Reagan announces his choice of liberal U.S. Senator Richard Schweiker as his vice presidential running mate, in an effort to woo moderate Republican delegates away from President Gerald Ford.
- July 27
  - The United Kingdom breaks diplomatic relations with its former colony Uganda in response to the hijacking of Air France Flight 139.
  - Delegates attending an American Legion convention at The Bellevue-Stratford Hotel in Philadelphia, US, begin falling ill with a form of pneumonia: this will eventually be recognised as the first outbreak of Legionnaires' disease and will end in the deaths of 29 attendees.
- July 28 – The Tangshan earthquake flattens Tangshan, China, killing 242,769 people, and injuring 164,851.
- July 29 – In New York City, the "Son of Sam" pulls a gun from a paper bag, killing 1 and seriously

wounding another, in the first of a series of attacks that terrorize the city for the next year.

- July 30 – In Santiago, Chile, Cruzeiro from Brazil beats River Plate from Argentina and are the Copa Libertadores de América champions.
- July 31
  - NASA releases the famous Face on Mars photo, taken by Viking 1.
  - The Big Thompson River in northern Colorado floods, destroying more than 400 cars and houses and killing 143 people.

## August

- August 1
  - The Caribbean nation of Trinidad and Tobago becomes a republic, replacing Elizabeth II with President Ellis Clarke as its head of state.
  - The Seattle Seahawks play their first football game.
  - Racing Champion Niki Lauda suffers serious burns in the German Grand Prix.
- August 2 – A gunman murders Andrea Wilborn and Stan Farr and injures Priscilla Davis and Gus Gavrel, in an incident at Priscilla's mansion in Fort Worth,

Texas. T. Cullen Davis, Priscilla's husband and one of the richest men in Texas, is tried and found innocent for Andrea's murder, involvement in a plot to kill several people (including Priscilla and a judge), and a wrongful death lawsuit. Cullen goes broke afterwards.

- August 5 – The Great Clock of Westminster (or Big Ben) suffers internal damage and stops running for over 9 months.
- August 6 – Former UK Postmaster General John Stonehouse is sentenced to 7 years' jail for fraud, theft and forgery.
- August 7 – Viking program: Viking 2 enters into orbit around Mars.
- August 8 – As part of the American Basketball Association–National Basketball Association merger, a dispersal draft was conducted to assign teams for the players on the two ABA franchises which had folded.
- August 11 – A sniper rampage in Wichita, Kansas on a Holiday Inn results in 3 deaths while 7 others are wounded.
- August 14
  - Ten thousand Protestant and Catholic women demonstrate for peace in Northern Ireland.

- The Senegalese political party *PAI-Rénovation* is legally recognized, becoming the third legal party in the country.
- August 16 – The Ramones make their first "professional" performance at CBGB.
- August 18 – At Panmunjom, North Korea, two United States soldiers are killed while trying to chop down part of a tree in the Korean Demilitarized Zone which had obscured their view.
- August 19 – U.S. President Gerald Ford edges out challenger Ronald Reagan to win the Republican Party presidential nomination in Kansas City.
- August 24 – In Uruguay, the army captures Marcelo Gelman and his pregnant wife. Marcelo is later killed and his wife (and unborn child) disappear.
- August 25
    - Jacques Chirac resigns as Prime Minister of France; he is succeeded by Raymond Barre.
    - Landslide disaster in Sau Mau Ping, Hong Kong.
- August 26
    - The first known outbreak of Ebola virus occurs in Yambuku, Zaire.
    - Prince Bernhard of Lippe-Biesterfeld, husband of Queen Juliana of the Netherlands, resigns from various posts over a scandal involving alleged

corruption, in connection with business dealings with the Lockheed Corporation.

- August 30 – James Alexander George Smith "Jags" McCartney is sworn in as the first Chief Minister of the Turks and Caicos Islands.

## September

- September 1
  - Cigarette and tobacco advertising is banned on Australian television and radio.
  - Aparicio Méndez, a jurist, is inaugurated as a civilian *de facto* President of Uruguay in the framework of a dictatorship.
  - The state of emergency, being in force since 1939, is lifted in the Republic of Ireland.
- September 3 – Viking program: The Viking 2 spacecraft lands at Utopia Planitia on Mars, taking the first close-up color photos of the planet's surface.
- September 6
  - Cold War: Soviet Air Force pilot Lt. Viktor Belenko lands a MiG-25 jet fighter at Hakodate, on the island of Hokkaidō in Japan, and requests political asylum in the United States.
  - Frank Sinatra brings Jerry Lewis's former partner Dean Martin onstage, unannounced, at the 1976 Jerry Lewis MDA Telethon in Las Vegas,

reuniting the comedy team for the first (and only) time in over 20 years.

- September 9 – Chairman Mao Zedong, of the People's Republic of China, dies of a heart attack.
- September 10
  - Zagreb mid-air collision: A British Airways Trident and a Yugoslav DC-9 collide near Zagreb, Yugoslavia (present-day Zagreb, Croatia), killing all 176 aboard.
  - Osamu Tezuka begins serialising *MW*, a manga inspired by the 1974 Kakuei Tanaka government scandal.
- September 13 – *The Muppet Show* is broadcast for the first time on ITV.
- September 16
  - Shavarsh Karapetyan saves 20 people from a trolleybus that had fallen into a Yerevan reservoir.
  - Beginning with the Night of the Pencils, a series of kidnappings and forced disappearances followed by torture, rape, and murder of students under the Argentine dictatorship takes place.
- September 17 – The space shuttle *Enterprise* is rolled out of a Palmdale, California hangar.

- September 20 – The International Organization of Space Communications (Intersputnik) is founded.
- September 20 – September 21 – The semi-legendary 100 Club Punk Festival ignites the careers of several influential punk and post-punk bands, arguably sparking the punk movement's introduction into mainstream culture.
- September 21
  - The Seychelles join the United Nations.
  - Orlando Letelier is assassinated in Washington, D.C. by agents of Chilean dictator Augusto Pinochet.
- September 24 – Patty Hearst is sentenced to 7 years in prison for her role in a 1974 bank robbery (an executive clemency order from U.S. President Jimmy Carter will set her free after only 22 months).
- September 25 – The Irish rock band U2 is formed after drummer Larry Mullen, Jr. posts a note seeking members for a band on the notice board of his Dublin school.
- September 28 – American singer Stevie Wonder releases his hit album *Songs in the Key of Life*.

# October

October 4: The InterCity 125 high-speed train is introduced in the UK; services begin two days later.

- October 4 – The brand new InterCity 125 high-speed train is introduced in the United Kingdom.
- October 6
  - Cubana de Aviación Flight 455 crashes due to a bomb placed by anti-Fidel Castro terrorists, after taking off from Bridgetown, Barbados; all 73 people on board are killed.
  - Students gathering at Thammasat University in Bangkok, Thailand are massacred, while protesting the return of ex-dictator Thanom Kittikachorn by a coalition of right-wing paramilitary and government forces, triggering the return of the military to government.
  - In San Francisco, during his second televised debate with Jimmy Carter, U.S. President Gerald Ford stumbles when he declares that "there is no

Soviet domination of Eastern Europe" (there is at the time).

- o The Cultural Revolution in China concludes upon the capture of the Gang of Four.
- October 8 – Thorbjörn Fälldin replaces Olof Palme as Prime Minister of Sweden .
- October 10 – Taiwan Governor Hsieh Tung-min is injured by a letter bomb from a pro-independence activist.
- October 12 – The People's Republic of China announces that Hua Guofeng is the successor to Mao Zedong, as Chairman of the Communist Party of China.
- October 13 – The United States Commission on Civil Rights releases the report, *Puerto Ricans in the Continental United States: An Uncertain Future*, that documents that Puerto Ricans in the United States have a poverty rate of 33 percent in 1974 (up from 29 percent in 1970), the highest of all major racial-ethnic groups in the country (not including Puerto Rico, a U.S. territory).
- October 18 – Ford officially launches volume production of the Fiesta car at its Valencia plant.
- October 19

- ○ The Copyright Act of 1976 extends copyright duration for an additional 20 years in the United States.
- ○ The Battle of Aishiya is fought in Lebanon.
- ○ The Chimpanzee (*Pan troglodytes*) is placed on the list of endangered species.
- October 20 – The Mississippi River ferry MV *George Prince* is struck by a ship while crossing from Destrehan, Louisiana to Luling, Louisiana, killing 78 passengers and crew.
- October 22 – Cearbhall Ó Dálaigh, the 5th President of Ireland, resigns after being publicly insulted by the Minister for Defense.
- October 25 – Clarence Norris, the last known survivor of the Scottsboro Boys, is pardoned.

### November

- November 2 – U.S. presidential election, 1976: Jimmy Carter defeats incumbent Gerald Ford, becoming the first candidate from the Deep South to win since the Civil War.
- November 15 – The first megamouth shark is discovered off Oahu in Hawaii.
- November 19 – Jaime Ornelas Camacho takes office as the first President of the Regional Government of Madeira, Portugal.

- November 24 – At least 3,840 are killed in a Richter scale magnitude 7.3 earthquake of Van and Muradiye in Turkey.
- November 25 – In San Francisco, The Band holds its farewell concert, *The Last Waltz*.
- November 26
  - Microsoft is officially registered with the Office of the Secretary of the State of New Mexico.
  - The Warsaw Treaty Organization joint secretariat is established.

## December

- December 1
  - Angola joins the United Nations.
  - José López Portillo takes office as President of Mexico.
  - The Sex Pistols achieve public notoriety, as they unleash several 4-letter words live on Bill Grundy's early evening TV show.
  - Sir Douglas Nicholls is appointed the 28th Governor of South Australia, the first Australian Aboriginal appointed to vice-regal office.
- December 3
  - Bob Marley and his manager Don Taylor are shot in an assassination attempt in Kingston, Jamaica.

- Patrick Hillery is elected unopposed as the 6th President of Ireland.
- December 6 – The Viet Cong is disbanded, and its former members become a part of the Vietnam People's Army.
- December 8
  - The Congressional Hispanic Caucus is established by the 5 Latinos in the United States Congress: Herman Badillo of the Bronx, E. de la Garza and Henry B. Gonzalez of Texas, Edward R. Roybal of California, and the nonvoting Resident Commissioner of Puerto Rico, Baltasar Corrada del Río.
  - *Hotel California* by the Eagles is released.
- December 10
  - The United Nations General Assembly adopts the Convention on the Prohibition of Military or Any Other Hostile Use of Environmental Modification Techniques.
  - The 9th Congress of the Sammarinese Communist Party convenes.
- December 15
  - Samoa joins the United Nations.
  - Denis Healey announces to the British Parliament that he has successfully negotiated a £2.3bn loan from the International Monetary Fund.

- December 20 – Richard J. Daley, Mayor of Chicago for 21 years, dies.
- December 23 – A new volcano, Murara, erupts in eastern Zaire.
- December 28 – Legendary guitarist Freddie King dies.

## Date unknown

- In late March 1976, the first truly complete recording of the opera *Porgy and Bess* is released in a 3-LP set, by Decca Records in England and by London Records in the U.S. It stars Willard White and Leona Mitchell. The orchestra is the Cleveland Orchestra conducted by Lorin Maazel.
- Random breath testing is introduced in Victoria (Australia).
- The first laser printer is introduced by IBM (the IBM 3800).
- California's sodomy law is repealed.
- The term memetics is first proposed by Richard Dawkins in his book *The Selfish Gene*.
- Diffie–Hellman key exchange cryptography is proposed.
- Plans to move the Nigerian capital from Lagos to Abuja are approved.
- The New Jersey Legislature passes legislation legalizing casinos in the shore town of Atlantic City

commencing in 1978. After signing the bill into law, Governor Brendan Byrne declares "The mob is not welcome in New Jersey!" referring to the Mafia's influence at casinos in Nevada.

- The Early Academic Outreach Program (EAOP) is established by the University of California (UC) in response to the State Legislature's recommendation to expand post-secondary opportunities to all of California's students including those who are first-generation, socioeconomically disadvantaged, and English-language learners.

# Births

## January

Phil Radford

Paz Vega

Johnny Yong Bosch

Emma Bunton

- January 2
  - Cletidus Hunt, American football player
  - Mahée Paiement, Canadian actress

- Phil Radford, American environmental, clean energy and democracy leader, Greenpeace Executive Director
- Paz Vega, Spanish actress
- January 4 – Shiro Amano, Japanese manga artist/writer
- January 5 – Shintarō Asanuma, Japanese voice actor
- January 6
  - Johnny Yong Bosch, American actor
  - Judith Rakers, German journalist and television presenter
- January 7
  - Éric Gagné, Canadian baseball player
  - Alfonso Soriano, Dominican baseball player
- January 8
  - Jenny Lewis, American actress and singer (Rilo Kiley)
  - Josh Meyers, American actor and comedian, brother of Seth Meyers
- January 10 – Adam Kennedy, American baseball player
- January 13
  - Ross McCall, Scottish actor
  - Michael Peña, American actor
  - Bic Runga, New Zealand singer/songwriter
  - Mario Yepes, Colombian football player

- January 19 – Marsha Thomason, English actress
- January 20
  - Kirsty Gallacher, Scottish TV presenter
  - Gretha Smit, Dutch speed skater
  - Anastasia Volochkova, Russian prima ballerina
  - Michael Myers, former NFL defensive tackle
- January 21 – Emma Bunton, English musician (Spice Girls)
- January 22
  - James Dearth, American football player
  - Mikko Luoma, Finnish ice-hockey player
- January 23
  - Angelica Lee, Taiwanese actress and singer
  - Nigel McGuinness, English professional wrestler
- January 27 – Clint Ford, American actor and writer
- January 28 – Mark Madsen, American basketball player
- January 30 – Andy Milonakis, American Internet and MTV star
- January 31
  - Buddy Rice, American race car driver
  - Paul Scheer, American actor and comedian

# February

Isla Fisher

Tony Jaa

Rashida Jones

- February 1 – Muteba Kidiaba, Congolese football goalkeeper
- February 2

- Carlos Coste, Venezuelan free-diver
- Lori Beth Denberg, American comedian
- James Hickman, British swimmer
- February 3
  - Isla Fisher, Australian actress
  - Tijana, Macedonian singer
- February 4 – Cam'ron, African-American rapper
- February 5
  - Abhishek Bachchan, Indian actor
  - Tony Jaa, Thai martial art film actor/choreographer/director
  - Brian Moorman, American football player
- February 6 – Kim Zmeskal, American Olympic gymnast
- February 9 – Charlie Day, American actor
- February 10 – Lance Berkman, American baseball player
- February 11 – Brice Beckham, American actor
- February 12
  - Jenni Falconer, British TV presenter
  - Silvia Saint, Czech actress
- February 14 – Erica Leerhsen, American actress
- February 15 – Brandon Boyd, American rock musician (Incubus)
- February 16 – Kyo, Japanese rock musician (Dir En Grey)

- February 17 – Svein Berge, Norwegian musician (Röyksopp)
- February 20
  - Johanna Beisteiner, Austrian guitarist
  - Chris Cillizza, American journalist
  - Gail Kim, Canadian professional wrestler
- February 21 – Michael McIntyre, British stand-up comedian
- February 23 – Jeff O'Neill, Canadian hockey player
- February 24 – Zach Johnson, American golfer
- February 25 – Rashida Jones, American actress, writer, model, and musician
- February 27 – Yukari Tamura, Japanese voice actress and songwriter
- February 28
  - Ali Larter, American actress and model
  - Guillaume Lemay-Thivierge, Canadian actor
- February 29 – Ja Rule, African-American rapper

## March

Haifa Wehbe

Reese Witherspoon

Peyton Manning

Corey Stoll

Keri Russell

- March 1 – Luke Mably, English actor
- March 3 – Fraser Gehrig, Australian rules footballer
- March 4
    - Robbie Blake, English footballer
    - Hiram Bocachica, Puerto Rican baseball player
    - Sean Covel, American film producer
    - Tommy Jönsson, Swedish football player
    - Regi Penxten, Belgian DJ and record producer
    - Thierry Renaer, Belgian field hockey player
- March 5 – Šarūnas Jasikevičius, Lithuanian basketball player
- March 6 – Ken Anderson, American professional wrestler (Mr. Anderson)
- March 8
    - Sergej Ćetković, Montenegrin singer
    - Gaz Coombes, English musician and singer-songwriter (Supergrass)
    - Freddie Prinze, Jr., American actor
- March 9 – Yamila Diaz-Rahi, Argentinean model
- March 10
    - Miroslav Kostadinov, Bulgarian singer and songwriter
    - Haifa Wehbe, Lebanese model, actress and singer
- March 12 – Zhao Wei, Chinese singer and actress
- March 13 – Danny Masterson, American actor
- March 14

- o Merlin Santana, American actor (d. 2002)
- o Corey Stoll, American actor
- March 16
  - o Blu Cantrell, American R&B singer
  - o Zhu Chen, Chinese chess grandmaster
  - o Pál Dárdai, Hungarian football player and manager
  - o Kim Johnsson, Swedish hockey player
- March 17
  - o Stephen Gately, Irish singer (Boyzone) (d. 2009)
  - o Álvaro Recoba, Uruguayan footballer
- March 19
  - o Rachel Blanchard, Canadian actress
  - o Alessandro Nesta, Italian football player
- March 20 – Chester Bennington, American singer (Linkin Park)
- March 21
  - o Dariush Ramezani, Iranian cartoonist
  - o Rachael MacFarlane, voice actress and singer, sister of Seth MacFarlane
- March 22
  - o Teun de Nooijer, Dutch field hockey player
  - o Wayne Turner, American basketball player
  - o Reese Witherspoon, American actress
- March 23
  - o Sir Chris Hoy, Scottish cyclist

- Keri Russell, American actress
- March 24
  - Aaron Brooks, American football player
  - Peyton Manning, American football player
- March 25 – Wladimir Klitschko, Ukrainian world heavyweight boxing champion
- March 26
  - Blaise Alexander, American automobile racing driver (d. 2001)
  - Amy Smart, American actress
- March 27 – Carl Ng, Hong Kong/British actor and model
- March 29 – Daisuke Namikawa, Japanese voice actor
- March 30
  - Jessica Cauffiel, American actress and singer
  - Ty Conklin, American ice-hockey player
  - Ayako Kawasumi, Japanese voice actress
- March 31 – Vice Ganda, Filipino actor and singer

## April

Melissa Joan Hart

Shu Qi

Tim Duncan

- April 2
    - Lucy Diakovska, German-Bulgarian pop singer
    - Rory Sabbatini, South African golfer
- April 3 – Will Mellor, English actor
- April 4 – James Roday, American actor, director and screenwriter
- April 5 – Henrik Stenson, Swedish golfer
- April 6 – Candace Cameron, American actress
- April 9 – Kris Radlinski, English rugby league player
- April 10 – Jan Werner Danielsen, Norwegian singer (d. 2006)

- April 12 – Andrei Lipanov, Russian ice skater
- April 13 – Yoo Ji-tae, South Korean actor
- April 13
  - Glenn Howerton, American actor
  - Jonathan Brandis, American actor (d. 2003)
- April 14 – Anna DeForge, American basketball player
- April 15
  - Jason Bonsignore, Canadian ice-hockey player
  - Brock Huard, former American football player
  - Steve Williams, British rower
- April 16 – Shu Qi, Taiwanese actress and singer
- April 17 – Kim Young-oh, South Korean illustrator
- April 18
  - Melissa Joan Hart, American actress
  - Sean Maguire, British actor and singer
- April 20 – Joey Lawrence, American actor
- April 21 – Rommel Adducul, Filipino basketball player
- April 22 – Michał Żewłakow, Polish footballer
- April 23 – Darren Huckerby, English footballer
- April 25
  - Tim Duncan, American basketball player
  - Rainer Schüttler, German tennis player
  - Kim Jong-kook, South Korean singer, TV personality

- April 29 – Jay Orpin, Swedish composer and record producer
  - Shiho Kawaragi, Japanese voice actress

**May**

Jeff Halpern

Colin Farrell

- May 3
  - Beto, Portuguese footballer
  - Jeff Halpern, American ice hockey player
- May 4 – Jason Michaels, American baseball player
- May 7

- Michael P. Murphy, U.S. Navy SEAL, First recipient of the Medal of Honor in the Afghanistan War
- Mariana van Zeller, Portuguese journalist and National Geographic correspondent
- May 8
  - Martha Wainwright, Canadian-American folk-pop singer
  - Ian Watkins, Welsh singer (Steps) and actor
- May 10 – Udo Mechels, Belgian singer
- May 14 – Martine McCutcheon, British actress and singer
- May 15
  - Tyler Walker, American baseball player
  - Jacek Krzynówek, Polish footballer
  - Ryan Leaf, American former football quarterback
- May 17 – Daniel Komen, Kenyan athlete
- May 19 – Kevin Garnett, American basketball player
- May 20 – Ramón Hernández, Venezuelan baseball player
- May 22
  - Chris Brazzell, Canadian and American Football player
  - Daniel Erlandsson, Swedish drummer
- May 25
  - Stefan Holm, Swedish high jumper

- ◦ Miguel Tejada, Dominican baseball player
- ◦ Cillian Murphy, Irish actor
- ◦ J. Michael Tatum, American voice actor
- ◦ Erinn Hayes, American actress
- May 26 – Paul Collingwood, English cricketer
- May 28
  - ◦ Alexei Nemov, Russian gymnast
  - ◦ Liam O'Brien, American actor
- May 31
  - ◦ Roar Ljøkelsøy, Norwegian ski jumper
  - ◦ Colin Farrell, Irish actor

## June

Lindsay Davenport

- June 1 – Angela Perez Baraquio, Miss America 2001
- June 2
  - ◦ Antônio Rodrigo Nogueira, Brazilian mixed martial artist

- Tim Rice-Oxley, English rock musician/composer (Keane)
- Queen 'Masenate Mohato Seeiso of Lesotho
- June 3 – Jamie McMurray, American race car driver
- June 5 – Ian Bavitz (Aesop Rock), American hip-hop artist
- June 6
  - Emilie-Claire Barlow, Canadian actress and singer
  - Geoff Rowley, English skateboarder
- June 8 – Lindsay Davenport, American tennis player
- June 9 – Ameesha Patel, Indian actress
- June 10
  - Freddy García, Venezuelan baseball player
  - Esther Ouwehand, Dutch politician, parliamentarian for the Party for the Animals
  - Mariana Seoane, Mexican actress
- June 11 – Gran Naniwa, Japanese professional wrestler
- June 13
  - Kym Marsh, British singer (Hear'Say) and actress
  - Jason "J" Brown, British singer (5ive)
- June 14 – Alan Carr, English comedian
- June 17 – Peter Svidler, Russian chess grandmaster
- June 18 – Blake Shelton, American singer
- June 20 – Juliano Haus Belletti, Brazilian footballer

- June 21 – Antonio Cochran, American football player
- June 23
  - Brandon Stokley, American football player
  - Emmanuelle Vaugier, Canadian actress
  - Patrick Vieira, French footballer
- June 26 – Chad Pennington, American football quarterback

## July

Bérénice Bejo

Adrien Grenier

Elsa Pataky

Benedict Cumberbatch

- July 1
  - Justin Lo, Hong Kong singer and actor
  - Patrick Kluivert, Dutch footballer
  - Ruud van Nistelrooy, Dutch footballer
  - Lina Rafn, Danish singer
  - Kellie Bright, English actress
- July 2 – Krisztián Lisztes, Hungarian footballer
- July 3
  - Shane Lynch, Irish singer (Boyzone)
  - Wanderlei Silva, Brazilian mixed martial artist

- July 4 – Daijiro Kato, Japanese motorcycle racer (d. 2003)
- July 5 – Nuno Gomes, Portuguese footballer
- July 7 – Bérénice Bejo, Argentine actress
- July 8 – Ellen MacArthur, English yachtswoman
- July 9
  - Shelton Benjamin, American professional wrestler
  - Mickey He, Chinese actor and singer
  - Fred Savage, American actor and director
- July 10
  - Ludovic Giuly, French footballer
  - Adrian Grenier, American actor, musician, and director
- July 11 – Eduardo Nájera, Mexican basketball player
- July 12 – Tracie Spencer, American R&B singer
- July 13 – Lisa Riley, British actress and presenter
- July 15 – Diane Kruger, German actress
- July 16
  - Anna Smashnova, Israeli tennis player
  - Bobby Lashley, American professional wrestler
- July 17
  - Luke Bryan, American country music singer-songwriter
  - Marcos Senna, Brazilian footballer
- July 18 – Elsa Pataky, Spanish actress

- July 19
  - Benedict Cumberbatch, English actor
  - Eric Prydz, Swedish DJ and producer
- July 20 – Alex Yoong, Malaysian race car driver
- July 23 – Judit Polgár, Hungarian chess player
- July 25
  - Mauricio Aspe, Mexican actor
  - Timur Mutsurayev, Chechen bard
  - Stéphane Rideau, French actor
- July 26 – Martha Roby, American U.S. Representative for Alabama's 2nd congressional district
- July 27 – Susanne Georgi, Danish singer who lives and works in Andorra
- July 28 – Jacoby Shaddix, American singer
- July 31
  - Annie Parisse, American actress
  - Mela Lee, American singer and voice actress

**August**

Sam Worthington

Soleil Moon Frye

- August 1
  - Nwankwo Kanu, Nigerian Football player
  - Amar Upadhyay, Indian television actor and model
  - Don Hertzfeldt, American animator
- August 2 – Sam Worthington, English-born Australian actor
- August 3
  - Troy Glaus, American baseball player
  - Mitch Jeffcoat, American programmer \ analyst \ engineer and screenwritter
- August 6
  - Soleil Moon Frye, American actress
  - Melissa George, Australian actress
- August 8
  - Drew Lachey, American singer (98 Degrees)
  - JC Chasez, American singer ('N Sync)
- August 9

- Aled Haydn Jones, Welsh radio producer and presenter
  - Mark Priestley, Australian actor (d. 2008)
  - Audrey Tautou, French actress
- August 11 – Will Friedle, American actor and comedian
- August 12
  - Mikko Lindström, Finnish rock guitarist
  - Antoine Walker, American basketball player
  - Wednesday 13, American rock musician
- August 14
  - Alex Albrecht, American television personality
  - Maya Nasri, Lebanese actress and singer
- August 15 – Boudewijn Zenden, Dutch football player
- August 18
  - Bryan Volpenhein, American rower
  - Lee Seung-yeop, South Korean baseball player
- August 19 – Michael M. Wartella, American underground cartoonist
- August 24 – Yang Yang, Chinese short track skater
- August 27
  - Carlos Moyá, Spanish tennis player
  - Mark Webber, Australian race car driver
  - Sarah Chalke, Canadian actress
- August 30
  - Lillo Brancato, Jr., American actor

○ Cristian Gonzáles, Uruguayan-born Indonesian footballer

## September

Naomie Harris

Ronaldo

Chiara Siracusa

- September 1
  - Marcos Ambrose Australian race car driver
  - Ivano Brugnetti, Italian race walker
- September 3
  - Jevon Kearse, American football player
  - Vivek Oberoi, Indian actor
- September 4 – Brian Myrow, American baseball player
- September 5 – Carice van Houten, Dutch actress
- September 6 – Naomie Harris, British actress
- September 7 – Stevie Case, American video game celebrity
- September 8 – Sjeng Schalken, Dutch tennis player
- September 9 – Lúcia Moniz, Portuguese singer and actess
- September 10 – Gustavo Kuerten, Brazilian tennis player
- September 12 – Maciej Żurawski, Polish footballer
- September 16 – Tina Barrett, English singer (S Club 7)
- September 17 – Kristian Kiehling, German-Latvian actor
- September 19
  - Isha Koppikar, Indian actress
  - Alison Sweeney, American actress
- September 20
  - Jon Bernthal, American actor

- Yui Horie, Japanese voice actress
- Enuka Okuma, Canadian actress
- September 22 – Ronaldo, Brazilian footballer
- September 23 – Rob James-Collier, British actor and model
- September 24 – Stephanie McMahon-Levesque, American wrestling promoter
- September 25
  - Chauncey Billups, American basketball player
  - Chiara Siracusa, Maltese singer, Eurovision Song Contest 2005 runner-up
- September 26 – Michael Ballack, German footballer
- September 27 – Francesco Totti, Italian footballer
- September 28 – Fedor Emelianenko, Russian mixed martial arts fighter
- September 29 – Andriy Shevchenko, Ukrainian footballer

## October

Nick Swardson

Emily Deschanel

Ryan Reynolds

- October 1 – Dora Venter, Hungarian pornographic actress
- October 4
  - Alicia Silverstone, American actress
  - Mauro Camoranesi, Italian footballer
- October 6
  - Barbie Hsu, Taiwanese actress and singer
  - Freddy García, Venezuelan baseball player
- October 7
  - Pekka Kuusisto, Finnish violinist
  - Taylor Hicks, American singer

- ○ Gilberto Silva, Brazilian football player
- October 9 – Nick Swardson, American actor and stand-up comedian
- October 10
  - ○ Bob Burnquist, Brazilian skateboarder
  - ○ Shane Doan, Canadian ice hockey player
- October 11 – Emily Deschanel, American actress
- October 14 – Chang Chen, Taiwanese actor
- October 15 – Yoon Son-ha, South Korean actress
- October 18 – Galder, Norwegian musician
- October 19
  - ○ Ryuji Imada, Japanese golfer
  - ○ Dan Smith, Canadian ice-hockey player
  - ○ Michael Young, American baseball player
  - ○ Desmond Harrington, American actor
- October 20 – Plamen Goranov, Bulgarian photographer, mountain climber and a Varna-based local protest leader (d. 2013)
- October 21 – Jeremy Miller, American actor
- October 23
  - ○ Cat Deeley, British television presenter
  - ○ Ryan Reynolds, Canadian actor
- October 25 – Steve Jones, Northern Irish footballer
- October 26
  - ○ Miikka Kiprusoff, Finnish hockey player
  - ○ Jeremy Wotherspoon, Canadian speed skater

- October 29 – Stephen Craigan, Northern Irish footballer

## November

Anna Faris

- November 1 – Chad Lindberg, American actor
- November 5 – Sean Brown, Canadian ice-hockey player
- November 6
  - Pat Tillman, American footballer (d. 2004)
  - Troy Hambrick, American football player
  - Wiley Wiggins, American actor
- November 7 – Mark Philippoussis, Australian tennis player
- November 8 – Brett Lee, Australian cricket player
- November 11 – Mike Leon Grosch, German singer
- November 12 – Mirosław Szymkowiak, Polish footballer
- November 16 – Mario Barravecchia, Italian singer

- November 17 – Diane Neal, American actress
- November 18 – Shagrath, Norwegian black metal musician (Dimmu Borgir)
- November 19
  - Jack Dorsey, American software architect, businessman, creator of Twitter
  - Jun Shibata, Japanese singer and songwriter
  - Robin Dunne, Canadian actress
- November 20
  - Laura Harris, Canadian actress
  - Dominique Dawes, African-American Olympic gymnast
- November 22
  - Torsten Frings, German footballer
  - Ville Valo, Finnish rock singer (HIM)
- November 24
  - Chen Lu, Chinese figure skater
  - Christian Laflamme, Canadian ice-hockey player
- November 25 – Grégory Havret, French golfer
- November 26 – Maia Campbell, American actress and singer
- November 27 – Jaleel White, African-American actor
- November 28 – Monster, guitarist (Mayday)
- November 29 – Anna Faris, American actress
- November 30 – Marco Castro, Peruvian-American director and cinematographer

# December

Dominic Monaghan

Armin van Buuren

Joe Manganiello

Danny McBride

- December 1 – Matthew Shepard, American murder victim (d. 1998)
- December 3
    - Cornelius Griffin, American football player
    - Marcos Denner, Brazilian footballer
- December 4 – Kristina Groves, Canadian speed skater
- December 6 – Alicia Machado, Miss Universe 1996
- December 7
    - Georges Laraque, Canadian ice-hockey player
    - Mark Duplass, American actor, screenwriter, and director
- December 8 – Dominic Monaghan, English actor
- December 13 – Radosław Sobolewski, Polish footballer
- December 14 – Leland Chapman, American bail bondsman
- December 15 – Baichung Bhutia, Indian footballer
- December 17 – Takeo Spikes, American football player

- December 18
  - Antti Koivumäki, Finnish poet and keyboardist (Aavikko) (d. 2002)
  - Koyuki, Japanese actress
- December 23 – Jamie Noble, American professional wrestler
- December 24 – Ángel Matos, Cuban former taekwondo athlete
- December 25
  - Tuomas Holopainen, Finnish metal keyboardist (Nightwish)
  - Armin van Buuren, Dutch music producer and DJ
- December 27 – Fernando Pisani, Canadian ice-hockey player
- December 28 – Joe Manganiello, American actor
- December 29 – Danny McBride, American actor and stand-up comedian

## Date unknown

- Bozorgmehr Hosseinpour, Iranian cartoonist

# Deaths

## January

Agatha Christie

Paul Robeson

- January 5 – John A. Costello, former Taoiseach of the Republic of Ireland (b. 1891)
- January 6 – Martha Walter, American impressionist painter (b. 1875)
- January 8 – Zhou Enlai, Premier of the People's Republic of China (b. 1898)
- January 10 – Howlin' Wolf, African-American musician (b. 1910)

- January 12 – Agatha Christie, English writer (*Murder On The Orient Express*) (b. 1890)
- January 13 – Margaret Leighton, English actress (b. 1922)
- January 15 – Gengo Hyakutake, Japanese admiral (b. 1882)
- January 19 – Hidetsugu Yagi, Japanese electrical engineer (b. 1886)
- January 21 – John Gould Moyer, American naval officer, 31st Governor of American Samoa (b. 1893)
- January 23 – Paul Robeson, African-American actor, singer, writer, and activist (b. 1898)
- January 26
  - Luis Alberti, Dominican Republic musician (b. 1906)
  - João Branco Núncio, Portuguese bullfighter (b. 1901)
- January 27 – Kaneko Daiei, Japanese Buddhist philosopher of the early 20th century (b. 1881)
- January 29 – James Edmonson, American vaudevillian and comedian (b. 1910)
- January 30
  - Mance Lipscomb, American singer (b. 1895)
  - Ernest Gold, British meteorologist and educated at St John's College, Cambridge (b. 1881)

- January 31 – Ernesto Miranda, American defendant in the court case *Miranda v. Arizona* (b. 1941)

## February

Werner Heisenberg

- February 1
  - Werner Heisenberg, German physicist, Nobel Prize laureate (b. 1901)
  - Hans Richter, German artist (b. 1888)
  - George Whipple, American scientist, recipient of the Nobel Prize in Physiology or Medicine (b. 1878)
- February 2 – Zlatyu Boyadzhiev, Bulgarian painter (b. 1903)
- February 4 – Roger Livesey, Welsh actor (b. 1906)
- February 6 – Vince Guaraldi, American musician (*Linus and Lucy*) (b. 1928)

- February 7 – Eliyahu Kitov, Jewish political activist (b. 1912)
- February 9 – Percy Faith, Canadian-born musician and composer (b. 1908)
- February 10 – Eddie Moore, American profession baseball player; 1925 World Series Champion (Pittsburgh Pirates) (b. 1899)
- February 11
  - Lee J. Cobb, American actor (b. 1911)
  - John H. Hester, American general (b. 1886)
  - Alexander Lippisch, German aerodynamicist (b. 1894)
  - Charlie Naughton, Scottish actor (b. 1886)
- February 12 – Sal Mineo, American actor (b. 1939)
- February 13
  - Lily Pons, American soprano (b. 1898)
  - John Lounsbery, American animator and director (b. 1911)
- February 17
  - Jean Servais, Belgian actor (b. 1910)
  - Marjorie Muir Worthington, American writer (b. 1900)
- February 18 – Joseph Henabery, American actor (b. 1888)
- February 20

- ○ René Cassin, French judge, recipient of the Nobel Peace Prize (b. 1887)
  - ○ Kathryn Kuhlman, American evangelist and faith healer (b. 1907)
- February 22 – Florence Ballard, American singer (*The Supremes*) (b. 1943)
- February 23 – L. S. Lowry, British artist (b. 1887)
- February 26 – Joseph Weil, American con man; nicknamed the "Yellow Kid" (b. 1875)
- February 29 – Grover Loening, American aircraft manufacturer (b.1888)

### March

Walter H. Schottky

Luchino Visconti

- March 4 – Walter H. Schottky, German physicist (b. 1886)
- March 5
  - Charles Lederer, American screenwriter (b. 1910)
  - Otto Tief, Estonian politician and military commander (b. 1889)
- March 6
  - Mary Petty, American illustrator (b. 1899)
  - Max 'Slapsie Maxie' Rosenbloom, American boxer and actor (b. 1907)
- March 7
  - Wright Patman, American politician (b. 1893)
  - Adolphe Reymond, Swiss football (b. 1896)
- March 8 – Alfons Rebane, Estonian military commander (b. 1908)

Marshal Bernard Montgomery

- March 10
  - Andris Andreiko, Latvian draughts player (b. 1942)

- Salomon Smolianoff, Russian counterfeiter and Holocaust survivor (b. 1899)
- Haddon Sundblom, Swedish illustrator and American artist (b. 1899)
- March 13 – Ernst Friedrich Löhndorff, German sailor, adventurer, and writer (b. 1899)
- March 14 – Busby Berkeley, American choreographer and director (b. 1895)
- March 17 – Luchino Visconti, Italian theatre and film director (b. 1906)
- March 19
  - Paul Kossoff, British rock guitarist (*Free*) (b. 1950)
  - Stuart Cloete, South African novelist, essayist, biographer and short story writer (b. 1897)
- March 24
  - Bernard Montgomery, British field marshal (b. 1887)
  - E. H. Shepard, English artist and book illustrator (b. 1879)
  - Francis Dominic Murnaghan, Irish mathematician (b. 1893)
- March 25 – Josef Albers, German-American artist (b. 1888)
- March 28 – Richard Arlen, American actor (b. 1899)
- March 31 – Paul Strand, American photographer (b. 1890)

# April

Howard Hughes

- April 1 – Max Ernst, German artist (b. 1891)
- April 4 – Harry Nyquist, American information theory pioneer (b. 1889)
- April 5 – Howard Hughes, American aviation pioneer, film director, and eccentric (b. 1905)
- April 9
  - Dagmar Nordstrom, American composer, pianist (*Nordstrom Sisters*) (b. 1903)
  - Phil Ochs, American folk singer and political activist (*Outside of a Small Circle of Friends*) (b. 1940)
- April 12
  - Miriam Cooper, American actress (b. 1891)
  - Paul Ford, American actor (b. 1901)
- April 14 – Maudie Prickett, American actress (b. 1914)
- April 18 – Henrik Dam, Danish biochemist, recipient of the Nobel Prize in Physiology or Medicine (b. 1895)

- April 22 – Michael Hole, American jockey (b. 1941)
- April 24
    - Mark Tobey, American painter (b. 1890)
    - Arvid Noe, Norwegian sailor and truck driver, probably the first European to die of AIDS-related illness (b. 1946)
- April 25
    - Carol Reed, English film director (b. 1906)
    - Markus Reiner, Israeli scientist (b. 1886)
    - Naum Shusterman, Soviet military engineer (b. 1912)
- April 26 – Sid James, South African actor (b. 1913)
- April 28 – Hilde Hildebrand, German actress (b. 1897)

**May**

Martin Heidegger

- May 1 – T. R. M. Howard, African-American civil rights leader and surgeon (b. 1908)

- May 3 – Ernie Nevers, American football player (Chicago Cardinals) and a member of the Pro Football Hall of Fame (b. 1902)
- May 9
  - Jens Bjørneboe, Norwegian author (b. 1920)
  - Ulrike Meinhof, German terrorist (b. 1934)
- May 11 – Alvar Aalto, Finnish architect (b. 1898)
- May 14 – Keith Relf, British rock musician (*The Yardbirds*) (b. 1943)
- May 20
  - Royal E. Ingersoll, American admiral (b. 1883)
  - Zelmar Michelini, Uruguayan politician, member of the Christian-Democrat party (disappeared) (b. 1924)
  - Héctor Gutiérrez Ruiz, Uruguayan politician (assassinated) (b. 1934)
- May 23 – Henry Cecil Leon, British novelist and lawyer (b. 1902)
- May 26
  - Martin Heidegger, German philosopher (b. 1889)
  - Juan Maino, Chilean leader of MAPU, "disappeared"
- May 27 – Ruth McDevitt, American actress (b. 1895)
- May 28 – Steffan Danielsen, Faroese painter (b. 1922)
- May 30

- Max Carey, American baseball player (Pittsburgh Pirates) and a member in the MLB Hall of Fame (b. 1890)
- Mitsuo Fuchida, Japanese aviator, naval officer, and Christian evangelist (b. 1902)

- May 31
  - Martha Beall Mitchell, American wife of John N. Mitchell (b. 1918)
  - Jacques Monod, French biologist, recipient of the Nobel Prize in Physiology or Medicine (b. 1910)

## June

J. Paul Getty

- June 2
  - Juan José Torres, former President of Bolivia (assassinated in the frame of Operation Condor) (b. 1920)
  - Don Bolles, American newspaper reporter (assassinated) (b. 1928)

- June 6
  - J. Paul Getty, American industrialist, founder of Getty Oil (b. 1892)
  - Victor Varconi, Hungarian actor (b. 1891)
- June 7
  - Bobby Hackett, American jazz musician (b. 1915)
  - Shigetarō Shimada, admiral in the Imperial Japanese Navy during World War II (b. 1883)
- June 9 – Sybil Thorndike, British actress (b. 1882)
- June 10 – Adolph Zukor, Hungarian-born film producer (b. 1873)
- June 11
  - Chief Red Fox, nephew of famed Sioux war leader, Crazy Horse (b. 1870)
  - Toots Mondt, American WWF promoter (b. 1886)
- June 14 – Knud, Hereditary Prince of Denmark (b. 1900)
- June 15 – Jimmy Dykes, American baseball player and manager (b. 1896)
- June 17 – Francisco Urondo, Argentine writer (b. 1930)
- June 23 – DeHart Hubbard, American Olympic athlete (b. 1903)
- June 24 – Imogen Cunningham, American photographer (b. 1883)

- June 25 – Johnny Mercer, American songwriter (b. 1909)
- June 28 – Stanley Baker, British actor (b. 1928)
- June 30
  - Firpo Marberry, American baseball player (b. 1898)
  - Alberta Ramage Neely, the wife of former Governor of West Virginia Matthew M. Neely (b. 1880)

## July

Gustav Heinemann

- July 1
  - Anneliese Michel, German Catholic woman who was believed to be possessed by demons (b. 1952)
  - Zhang Wentian, General Secretary of the Communist Party of China (b. 1900)
- July 4
  - Yonatan Netanyahu, Israeli commando leader (b. 1946)

- Antoni Słonimski, Polish poet and writer (b. 1895)
- July 5 – Harold F. Loomis, American botanist and myriapodologist (b. 1896)
- July 6 – Zhu De, China Red Army Commander-in-Chief (b. 1886)
- July 7
  - Norman Foster, American film director (b. 1900)
  - Walter Giesler, American soccer coach (b. 1910)
  - Gustav Heinemann, former German president (b 1899)
  - Walter Lowenfels, American poet, journalist, and member of the Communist Party USA (b. 1897)
- July 8 – James Liston, 7th Roman Catholic Bishop of Auckland, New Zealand (b. 1881)
- July 11 – León de Greiff, Colombian poet (b. 1895)
- July 12
  - James Wong Howe, American cinematographer (b. 1899)
  - Ted Mack, American radio and television host (b. 1904)
- July 13
  - Frederick Hawksworth, GWR Chief mechanical engineer (b. 1884)
  - Joachim Peiper, German military leader (b. 1915)

- July 15 – Paul Gallico, American novelist, short story and sports writer (b. 1897)
- July 16 – Carmelo Soria, Spanish diplomat (assassinated by the Chilean DINA) (b. 1921)
- July 17 – Arthur Hornblow, Jr., American film producer (b. 1893)
- July 18 – Charles Howson, English professional footballer (b. 1896)
- July 20 – Max Maxudian, French stage and film actor (b. 1881)
- July 21 – Earle Combs, American baseball player (New York Yankees) and a member of the MLB Hall of Fame (b. 1899)
- July 22 – Sir Mortimer Wheeler, British archaeologist (b. 1890)
- July 24 – Afro Basaldella, Italian painter (b. 1912)
- July 29 – Mickey Cohen, American gangster (b. 1913)
- July 30 – Rudolf Bultmann, German Lutheran theologian (b. 1884)

# August

Fritz Lang, 1969

Juscelino Kubitschek

- August 2
  - Cecilia, Spanish singer-songwriter (b. 1948)
  - Fritz Lang, Austrian-German-American filmmaker, screenwriter and occasional film producer (b. 1890)
- August 3
  - Vladimir Vranić, Croatian mathematician (b. 1896)
  - Valery Sablin, Soviet mutineer (executed) (b. 1939)

- August 4 – Enrique Angelelli, Argentine bishop (assassinated in the "Dirty War") (b. 1923)
- August 6
  - Gregor Piatigorsky, Russian cellist (b. 1903)
  - Hans Edmund Nicola Burgeff, German botanist (b.1883)
  - William Mervyn, English actor (b.1912)
  - Charles Broad, British Army General during World War II (b.1882)
- August 10
  - Ray "Crash" Corrigan, American actor (b. 1902)
  - Robert L. May, Creator of Rudolph the Red-Nosed Reindeer (b. 1905)
- August 19 – Alastair Sim, Scottish actor (b. 1900)
- August 22 – Juscelino Kubitschek, President of Brazil (b. 1902)
- August 25 – Eyvind Johnson, Swedish writer, Nobel Prize laureate (b. 1900)
- August 26
  - Warner Anderson, American actor (b. 1911)
  - Lotte Lehmann, German soprano (b. 1888)
  - John Grimes, Archdeacon of Northampton from 1941 to 1959 (b. 1881)
- August 27 – Mukesh, Indian singer (b. 1923)
- August 28 – Anissa Jones, American actress (b. 1958)

# September

Mao Zedong

- September 2 – Stanisław Grochowiak, Polish writer (b. 1934)
- September 5 – Arthur Gilligan, English cricket captain (b. 1894)
- September 9
  - Yehezkel Abramsky, Russian-born rabbi, head of the London Beth Din for 17 years (b. 1886)
  - Mao Zedong, Chinese communist revolutionary, guerrilla warfare strategist, author, political theorist, and leader of the Chinese Revolution (b. 1893)
- September 10 – Dalton Trumbo, American screenwriter, one of the Hollywood Ten (b. 1905)
- September 14 – Prince Paul of Yugoslavia (b. 1893)
- September 15 – Josef Sudek Czech photographer, best known for his photographs of Prague (b. 1896)

- September 19 – Choe Yong-gon, North Korean general and defense minister (b. 1900)
- September 21 – Orlando Letelier, Chilean former minister of Salvador Allende (assassinated in Washington, D.C.) (b. 1932)
- September 25 – Red Faber, American baseball player (Chicago White Sox) and a member of the MLB Hall of Fame (b. 1888)
- September 26 – Lavoslav Ružička, Croatian chemist, Nobel Prize laureate (b. 1887)
- September 27 – Ivan Donald Margary, American historian (b. 1896)
- September 28 – Raymond Collishaw, Canadian World War I fighter ace (b. 1893)
- September 30 – Paul Dehn, British screenwriter (b. 1912)

## October

- October 4 – Leo Eloesser, American thoracic surgeon (b. 1881)
- October 5
  - Barbara Nichols, American actress (b. 1929)
  - Lars Onsager, Norwegian chemist, Nobel Prize laureate (b. 1903)
- October 6 – Gilbert Ryle, British philosopher (b. 1900)

- October 9 – Troy H. Middleton, American general and educator (b. 1889)
- October 11
    - Connee Boswell, American singer (b. 1907)
    - Alfredo Bracchi, Italian author (b. 1897)
- October 14 – Edith Evans, British actress (b. 1888)
- October 15 – Augusta Stevenson, writer of children's literature and a teacher (b. 1869)
- October 25 – Raymond Queneau, French poet and novelist (b. 1903)
- October 28 – Máire Drumm, Irish nationalist politician (assassinated) (b. 1919)
- October 31 – Eileen Gray, Irish furniture designer (b. 1878)

## November

Rosalind Russell

- November 6 – David Marine, American pathologist (b. 1888)

- November 7 – Grace Stone Coates, wrote short stories, novels, poetry, and news articles (b. 1881)
- November 8 – Gottfried von Cramm, German tennis champion (b. 1909)
- November 9 – Billy Halop, American actor (b. 1920)
- November 10 – Syd Coventry, Australian footballer (b. 1899)
- November 11 – Alexander Calder, American sculptor (b. 1898)
- November 12 – Walter Piston, American composer (b. 1894)
- November 15 – Jean Gabin, French actor (b. 1904)
- November 18 – Man Ray, American artist (b. 1890)
- November 19 – Wayne Millner, American football player (Washington Redskins) and a member of the Pro Football Hall of Fame (b. 1913)
- November 20 – Trofim Lysenko, Soviet biologist and agronomist of Ukrainian origin (b. 1898)
- November 21 – Walter Stuart Diehl, American naval officer and aeronautical engineer (b. 1893)
- November 23 – André Malraux, French writer and statesman (b. 1901)
- November 25 – Boris Zakhava, Russian theatre director, actor and acting coach (b. 1896)
- November 28
  - Rosalind Russell, American actress (b. 1907)

- Albert Caquot, considered as the "best living French engineer" (b. 1881)
- November 29
  - Godfrey Cambridge, American actor (b. 1933)
  - Judith Lowry, American actress (b. 1890)

### December

Benjamin Britten

João Goulart

- December 2 – Danny Murtaugh, American baseball player and manager (b. 1917)
- December 3
  - Angelo Iachino, Italian admiral (b. 1889)
  - Mary Nash, American actress (b. 1884)

- Louis E. Eliasberg, American financier and numismatist (b. 1896)
- December 4
  - Benjamin Britten, English composer (b. 1913)
  - Tommy Bolin, American guitarist (b. 1951)
- December 6 – João Goulart, President of Brazil (b. 1918)
- December 7 – Frank Forest, American operatic tenor and actor (b. 1896)
- December 8 – Henryk Jasiczek, Polish writer and political activist (b. 1919)
- December 9 – Mohamed El-Tabii, Egyptian political writer, journalist and a pioneer (b. 1896)
- December 12 – Jack Cassidy, American actor of stage, film, and screen (b. 1927)
- December 15 – Grégoire Kayibanda, former President of Rwanda (b. 1924)
- December 18 – Ned Harris, American baseball outfielder for Detroit Tigers (b. 1916)
- December 20 – Richard J. Daley, American Mayor of Chicago (b. 1902)
- December 21 – Thomas Simpson Crawford, Australian politician (b. 1875)
- December 24 – Duarte Nuno, Duke of Braganza, claimant to the throne of Portugal (b. 1907)
- December 25

- ○ Frankie Darro, American actor (b. 1917)
- ○ Irving Lerner, American cinematographer and director (b. 1909)
- ○ Frank R. Walker, American admiral (b. 1899)
- December 26 – Phil Hart, U.S. Senator (b. 1912)
- December 28 – Katharine Byron, U.S. Congresswoman (b. 1903)
- December 29 – Albert Salomon, German surgeon at the Royal Surgical University Clinic in Berlin (b. 1883)
- December 31 – Teohari Georgescu, Romanian politician (b. 1908)

## Date unknown

- Mariano Andreu, Spanish painter (b. 1888)
- Maria Klenova, Russian marine geologist (b. 1898)

# Nobel Prizes

- Physics – Burton Richter, Samuel Chao Chung Ting
- Chemistry – William Nunn Lipscomb, Jr
- Physiology or Medicine – Baruch S. Blumberg, D Carleton Gajdusek
- Literature – Saul Bellow
- Peace – Betty Williams and Mairead Corrigan
- Economics – Milton Friedman

# In the News.

**1976 Summer Olympics -** Montreal, Quebec, Canada.

Apple Computer was formed by Steve Jobs

**Best Film Oscar Winner –** Rocky

**1976 Most Popular TV shows:**

1. Happy Days
2. Laverne & Shirley
3. M*A*S*H
4. Charlie's Angels
5. The Big Event
6. The Six Million Dollar Man
7. Baretta
8. One Day at a Time
9. Three's Company
10. All in the Family

**Time Magazine's Man of the Year -** Jimmy Carter

The ink-jet printer is invented.

**1976's Most Popular Christmas gift-** Stretch Armstrong.

# 1976 Calendar.

## January 1976
| Sun | Mon | Tue | Wed | Thu | Fri | Sat |
|-----|-----|-----|-----|-----|-----|-----|
|     |     |     |     | 1   | 2   | 3   |
| 4   | 5   | 6   | 7   | 8   | 9   | 10  |
| 11  | 12  | 13  | 14  | 15  | 16  | 17  |
| 18  | 19  | 20  | 21  | 22  | 23  | 24  |
| 25  | 26  | 27  | 28  | 29  | 30  | 31  |

## February 1976
| Sun | Mon | Tue | Wed | Thu | Fri | Sat |
|-----|-----|-----|-----|-----|-----|-----|
| 1   | 2   | 3   | 4   | 5   | 6   | 7   |
| 8   | 9   | 10  | 11  | 12  | 13  | 14  |
| 15  | 16  | 17  | 18  | 19  | 20  | 21  |
| 22  | 23  | 24  | 25  | 26  | 27  | 28  |
| 29  |     |     |     |     |     |     |

## March 1976
| Sun | Mon | Tue | Wed | Thu | Fri | Sat |
|-----|-----|-----|-----|-----|-----|-----|
|     | 1   | 2   | 3   | 4   | 5   | 6   |
| 7   | 8   | 9   | 10  | 11  | 12  | 13  |
| 14  | 15  | 16  | 17  | 18  | 19  | 20  |
| 21  | 22  | 23  | 24  | 25  | 26  | 27  |
| 28  | 29  | 30  | 31  |     |     |     |

## April 1976
| Sun | Mon | Tue | Wed | Thu | Fri | Sat |
|-----|-----|-----|-----|-----|-----|-----|
|     |     |     |     | 1   | 2   | 3   |
| 4   | 5   | 6   | 7   | 8   | 9   | 10  |
| 11  | 12  | 13  | 14  | 15  | 16  | 17  |
| 18  | 19  | 20  | 21  | 22  | 23  | 24  |
| 25  | 26  | 27  | 28  | 29  | 30  |     |

## May 1976
| Sun | Mon | Tue | Wed | Thu | Fri | Sat |
|-----|-----|-----|-----|-----|-----|-----|
|     |     |     |     |     |     | 1   |
| 2   | 3   | 4   | 5   | 6   | 7   | 8   |
| 9   | 10  | 11  | 12  | 13  | 14  | 15  |
| 16  | 17  | 18  | 19  | 20  | 21  | 22  |
| 23  | 24  | 25  | 26  | 27  | 28  | 29  |
| 30  | 31  |     |     |     |     |     |

## June 1976
| Sun | Mon | Tue | Wed | Thu | Fri | Sat |
|-----|-----|-----|-----|-----|-----|-----|
|     |     | 1   | 2   | 3   | 4   | 5   |
| 6   | 7   | 8   | 9   | 10  | 11  | 12  |
| 13  | 14  | 15  | 16  | 17  | 18  | 19  |
| 20  | 21  | 22  | 23  | 24  | 25  | 26  |
| 27  | 28  | 29  | 30  |     |     |     |

## July 1976
| Sun | Mon | Tue | Wed | Thu | Fri | Sat |
|-----|-----|-----|-----|-----|-----|-----|
|     |     |     |     | 1   | 2   | 3   |
| 4   | 5   | 6   | 7   | 8   | 9   | 10  |
| 11  | 12  | 13  | 14  | 15  | 16  | 17  |
| 18  | 19  | 20  | 21  | 22  | 23  | 24  |
| 25  | 26  | 27  | 28  | 29  | 30  | 31  |

## August 1976
| Sun | Mon | Tue | Wed | Thu | Fri | Sat |
|-----|-----|-----|-----|-----|-----|-----|
| 1   | 2   | 3   | 4   | 5   | 6   | 7   |
| 8   | 9   | 10  | 11  | 12  | 13  | 14  |
| 15  | 16  | 17  | 18  | 19  | 20  | 21  |
| 22  | 23  | 24  | 25  | 26  | 27  | 28  |
| 29  | 30  | 31  |     |     |     |     |

## September 1976
| Sun | Mon | Tue | Wed | Thu | Fri | Sat |
|-----|-----|-----|-----|-----|-----|-----|
|     |     |     | 1   | 2   | 3   | 4   |
| 5   | 6   | 7   | 8   | 9   | 10  | 11  |
| 12  | 13  | 14  | 15  | 16  | 17  | 18  |
| 19  | 20  | 21  | 22  | 23  | 24  | 25  |
| 26  | 27  | 28  | 29  | 30  |     |     |

## October 1976
| Sun | Mon | Tue | Wed | Thu | Fri | Sat |
|-----|-----|-----|-----|-----|-----|-----|
|     |     |     |     |     | 1   | 2   |
| 3   | 4   | 5   | 6   | 7   | 8   | 9   |
| 10  | 11  | 12  | 13  | 14  | 15  | 16  |
| 17  | 18  | 19  | 20  | 21  | 22  | 23  |
| 24  | 25  | 26  | 27  | 28  | 29  | 30  |
| 31  |     |     |     |     |     |     |

## November 1976
| Sun | Mon | Tue | Wed | Thu | Fri | Sat |
|-----|-----|-----|-----|-----|-----|-----|
|     | 1   | 2   | 3   | 4   | 5   | 6   |
| 7   | 8   | 9   | 10  | 11  | 12  | 13  |
| 14  | 15  | 16  | 17  | 18  | 19  | 20  |
| 21  | 22  | 23  | 24  | 25  | 26  | 27  |
| 28  | 29  | 30  |     |     |     |     |

## December 1976
| Sun | Mon | Tue | Wed | Thu | Fri | Sat |
|-----|-----|-----|-----|-----|-----|-----|
|     |     |     | 1   | 2   | 3   | 4   |
| 5   | 6   | 7   | 8   | 9   | 10  | 11  |
| 12  | 13  | 14  | 15  | 16  | 17  | 18  |
| 19  | 20  | 21  | 22  | 23  | 24  | 25  |
| 26  | 27  | 28  | 29  | 30  | 31  |     |